The Laser Cutter Handbook

Eric Goodwin

Copyright © 2021 Eric Goodwin

All rights reserved.

ISBN:
ISBN-13:

DEDICATION

This book is dedicated to those budding entrepreneurs who buy machines and make wonderful things with them.

CONTENTS

	Acknowledgments	i
1	Introduction	8
2	How Laser Cutters Work	Pg 16
3	Buying Your First Machine	Pg 33
4	Setting Up Your Machine	Pg 37
5	The Design Software	Pg 39
6	Running a Test Project	Pg 48
7	Tools & Equipment	Pg 52
8	Essential Maintenance	Pg 59
9	Troubleshooting	Pg 63
10	Get Creative!	Pg 66
11	Useful Links	Pg 70

DISCLAIMER

The information contained in this book is for entertainment purposes only. The author and publisher of this information accept no liability for any loss or injury arising from the use or misuse of the information contained herein.

ACKNOWLEDGMENTS

I'd like to acknowledge those people who helped me put this book together, with a special mention for Rosie.

1 - INTRODUCTION

Welcome to the Laser Cutter Handbook and thank you for purchasing this guide. The idea for creating this book came from many months of searching for information on the various aspects of setting up a Laser Cutter for first use. I'm happy to pass on this hard won knowledge, in the hope that it helps to expedite your quest into laser cutter technology.

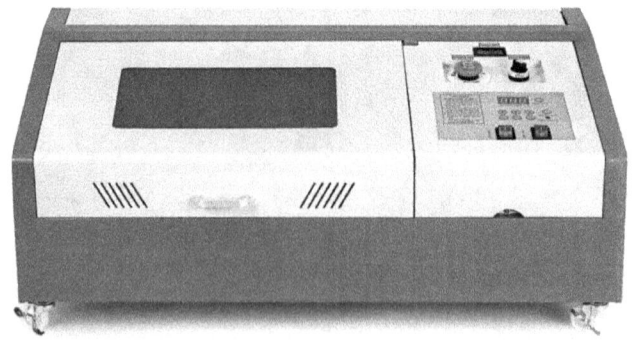

When I bought my first machine 10 years ago, the manufacturer's instructions it came with were written in Chinese and damn near useless. Contacting the UK supplier I purchased it from yielded very little in the way of support. So I then began searching the internet for anything that would help me, but there really wasn't much information out there to find, certainly not enough for a complete novice.

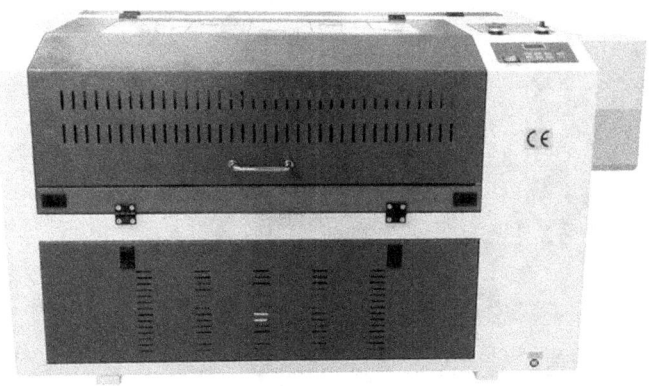

After struggling to find tiny scraps of information about these machines for myself, I believe that a real need exists for more information on how to set up and use a laser cutter. I hope this guide helps you in your search to find and purchase the right machine for your purpose; then you can start using this technology in a safe and productive way.

I believe that it's always best to research a new subject before you take the plunge, this approach will save you both time and money. The most sensible approach to any new endeavor is to first learn from other people's mistakes, because observing those mistakes won't cost you money!

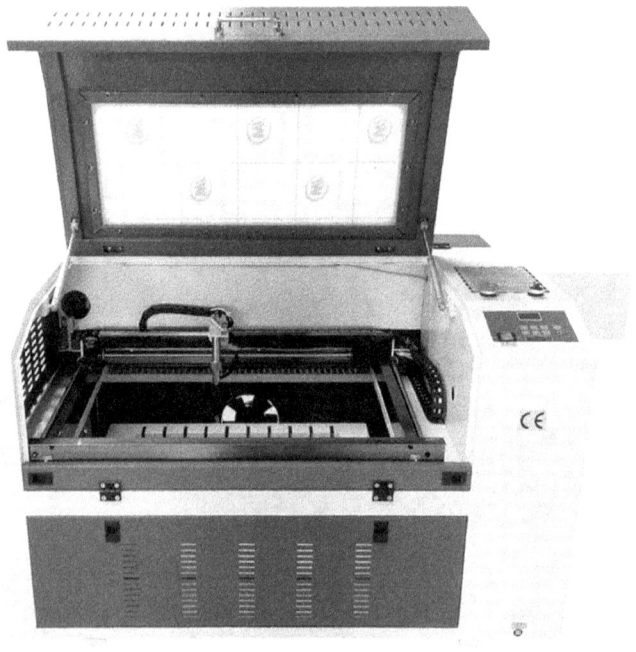

I became involved with CO2 laser cutting machinery and related equipment by necessity. My business was being equally squeezed by the suppliers and my competitors, I was caught between a rock and a hard place. If I wanted to stay in business, I had to start making my own products or else give up and close the shop. Well, I wasn't quite ready to accept defeat and I'd like to share my adventure with you, into the surprisingly undocumented world of Laser Cutting & Engraving Equipment.

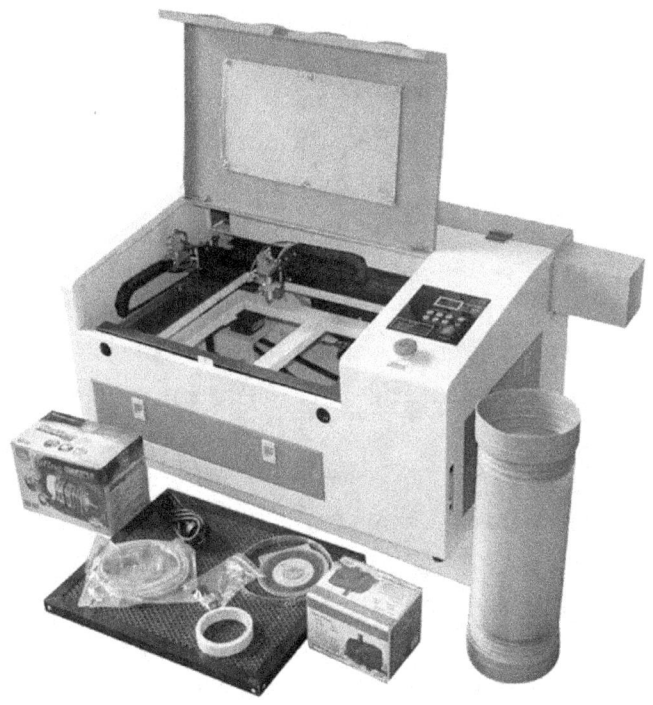

Ten years ago I started a retail business in the catering industry. Many of the products we sold were manufactured from Acrylic (Perspex) and Mylar sheets. Those products were mainly two and three dimensional templates and stencils, most were fairly simple designs.

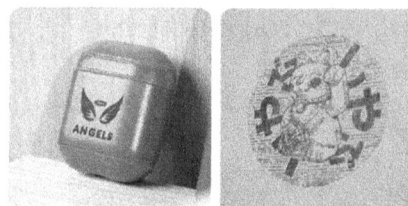 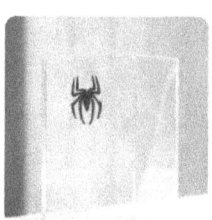

At that time we had plenty of options for wholesale suppliers of the products we stocked; but when it came to small quantities or custom designs, the high purchase costs made it unprofitable. So in an effort to circumvent high UK prices, I ventured into the world of Chinese manufacturers via Alibaba.com (for Wholesale) and its sister website Aliexpress.com (more retail orientated).

If you don't already know, those two websites I mentioned they are gateways to wholesale suppliers in many industries. I dabbled with them for a time, but it proved unproductive for my purposes, the quality was hit and miss to the extreme, with equally unpredictable delivery times. I often found myself waiting up to three months for the delivery of products which would frequently be not even close to what I'd ordered, it was a total lottery, and the odds were just not working in my favor. So I temporarily retreated back to the safety of my regular UK suppliers, and began to dig a little deeper into where these suppliers sourced their products.

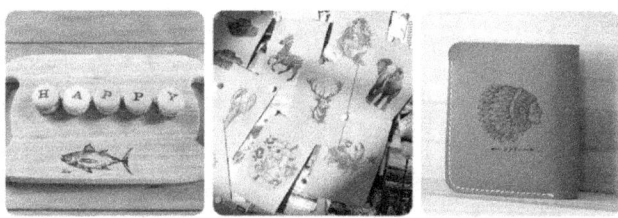

After further investigation, I discovered that many of them were utilizing laser cutting technology to create their products from scratch. That was the defining moment when I decided that it might just be worth the effort to experiment with a laser cutter and create my own products. So I hatched a plan to start it on a small scale and see how this technology works.

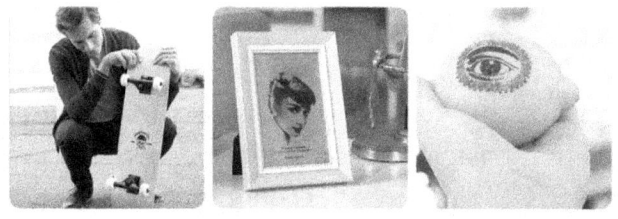

I have a background in electronic servicing and repair and have also previously worked in the computer industry, so initially it seemed like a reasonable proposition to manufacture my own unique products with a laser cutter, but it quickly became evident that I had so much to learn, it wasn't going to be the 'cake-walk' I'd first imagined.

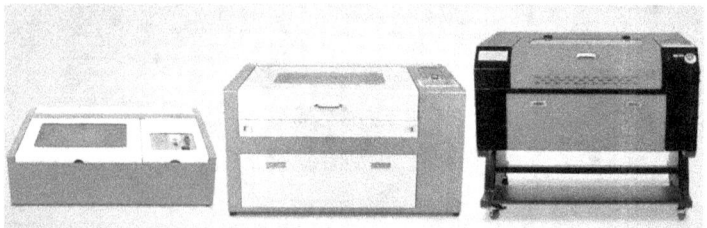

Having owned and operated machines in several different sizes, I have collected what I believe to be valuable information that will help you avoid the costly mistakes which can arise when becoming familiar with your laser cutting machine. In the following chapters I will provide all the tried and tested techniques I have used to create projects to an acceptable standard, which can then be safely used or sold.

The aim of this guide is to provide the novice user with a basic understanding of how to set up and use a CO_2 laser cutter/engraver. If the instructions contained within are followed carefully (without deviation), then it should enable you to start manufacturing your own products.

THE LASER CUTTER HANDBOOK

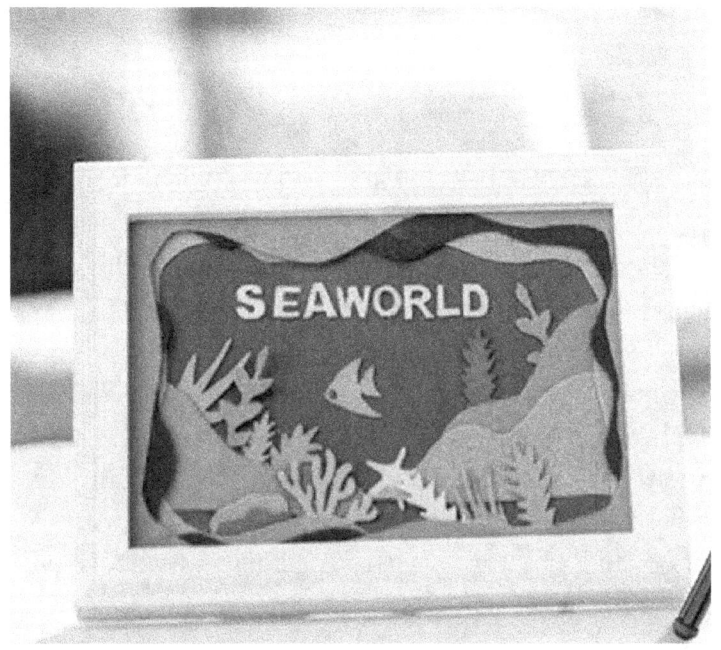

2 – HOW LASER CUTTERS WORK

A CO_2 laser cutting and engraving machine is used to cut out flat material into various shapes which can then be used to manufacture products or prototypes. There are many more advanced machines which can be combined with high specification software to create 3D carving on various types of material but this book is concerned mainly with a basic $Co2$ laser, although most of the principal techniques do transfer.

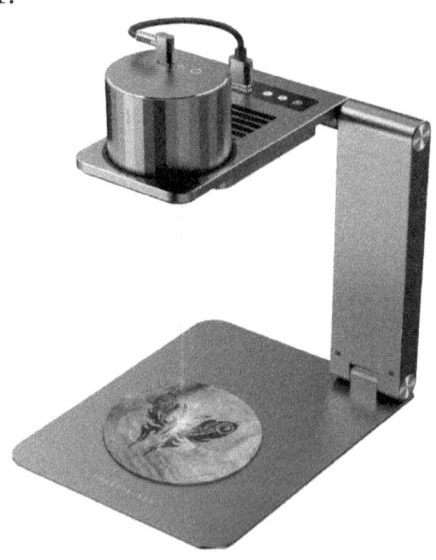

There also exists some small hobbyist machines (as shown in the previous & next images), but they really are not much use for any serious projects. If you plan to start any kind of business, you'll be making multiple products in succession, and that's exactly where these hobby machines fail to work properly. They will quickly overheat and destroy themselves if used for too long. There's also the issue of smoke and fumes during the cutting process of some materials.

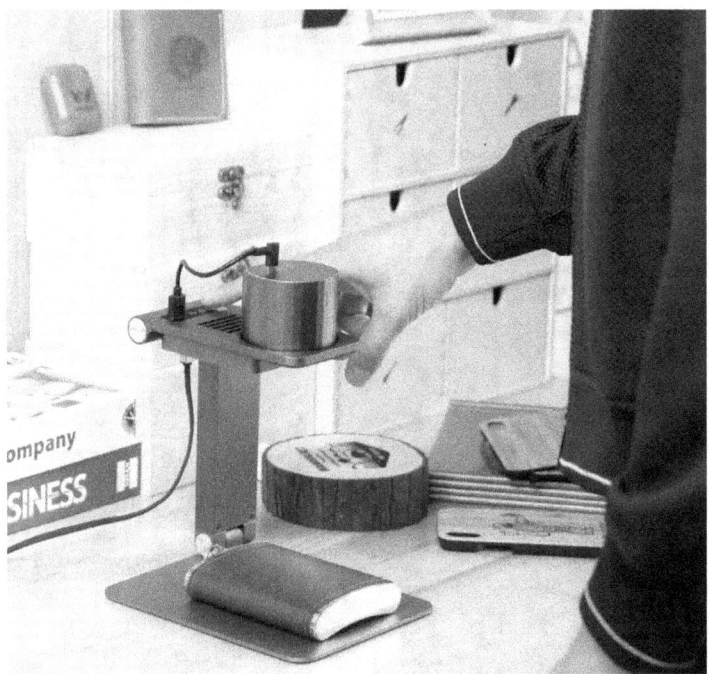

If you wish to make products all day long, then

you will need a sturdy machine complete will a proper cooling & fume extraction system, only then will it be truly safe to manufacture products for resale.

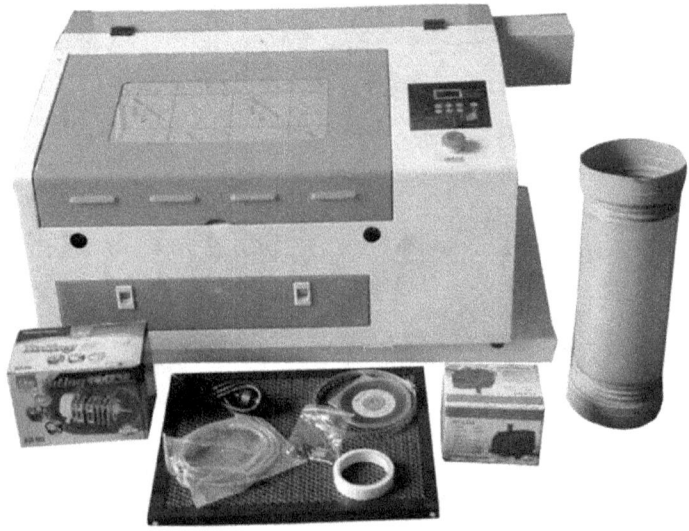

The main task at hand is to convert a digital design into a real world object which can then be utilized in some way, for example products for sale or use in your own workshop. I have created many different types of jigs for my table saw which just makes life a little bit easier when carrying out repetitive jobs.

THE LASER CUTTER HANDBOOK

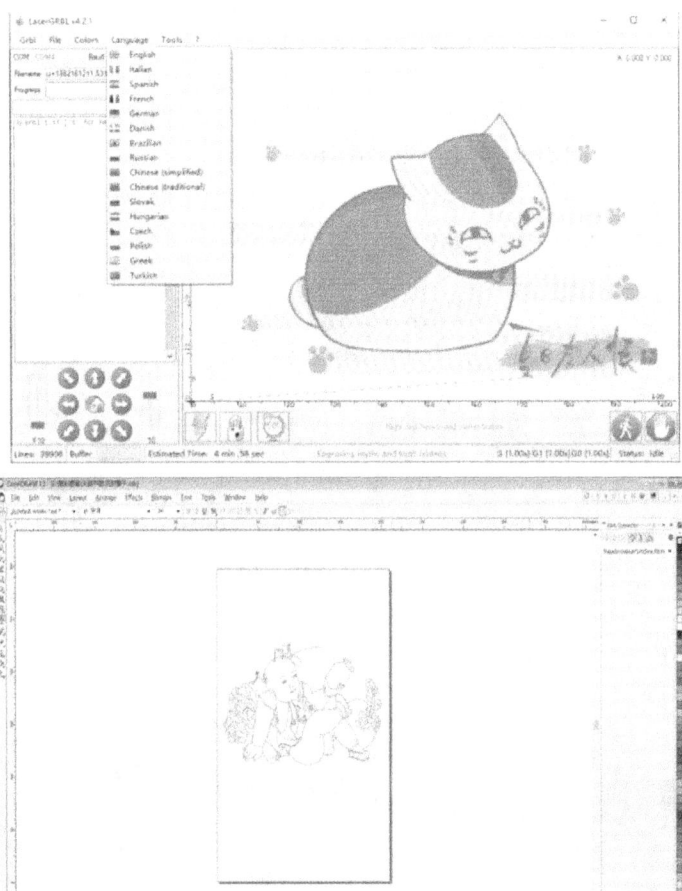

The laser machine can cut and engrave (raster) most materials which will be described later in this handbook. However they are not generally used for cutting any type of metal unless you are willing to invest in a more powerful costly machine which is used specifically for cutting metal. You can expect to pay GBP£60K+ for a medium range machine (in 2021).

It is possible to engrave onto metal surface with the CO2 laser, but you must apply a special tape or paste before starting any work, links provided for suppliers in chapter 11.

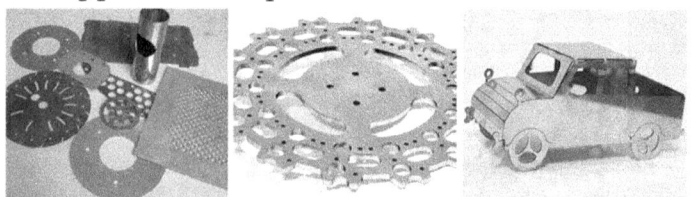

You can think of the laser machine as a type of CNC (computer numerical control) which basically means that it is controlled by a computer but it is also classed as a manufacturing tool and a rapid prototyping tool.

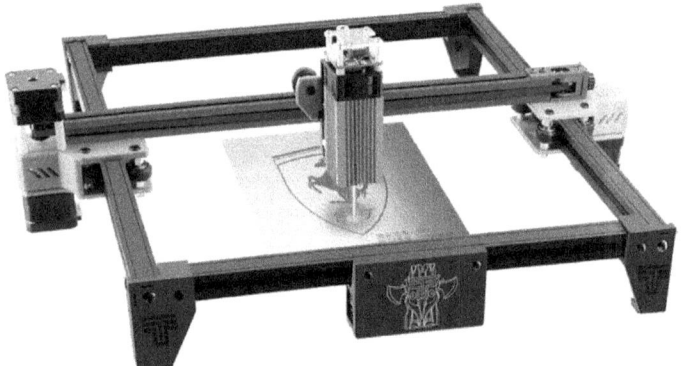

The basics of operation are to buy and install several pieces of hardware along with a connected computer and then use this in conjunction with various graphics software programs to control the output of the machine. Contained within the machine casing lies the main part of the machine, namely the glass tube or laser tube (laser resonator) which will originate a beam of light in the infra-red spectrum that is usually invisible to the naked eye.

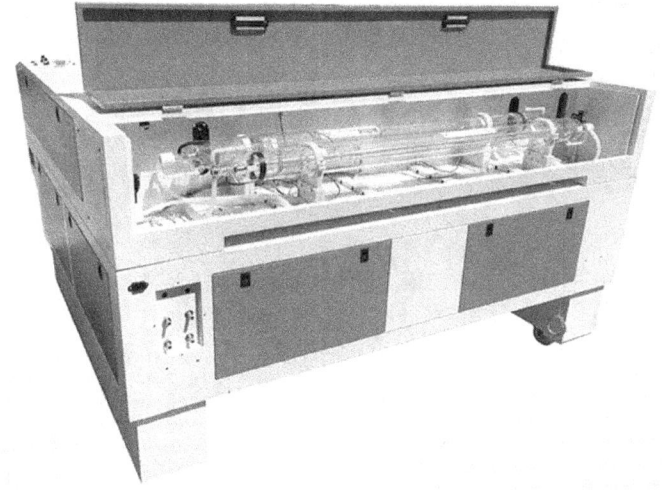

The beam is directed through a system of moving and static mirrors (flying optics) along to the cutting head. Within the cutting head the beam is then focused through a lens (meniscus) down to a thin concentrated beam of light which then hits the material and cuts it.

There are several types of RF laser tubes, including solid state versions which will cost upwards of GBP£6000 with a lifespan of 6000 –

10000 hours of use. They are air cooled instead of the water-cooled versions and are a lot noisier. Typically they can be re-gassed and re-installed at a cost of GBP£2500 (2021).

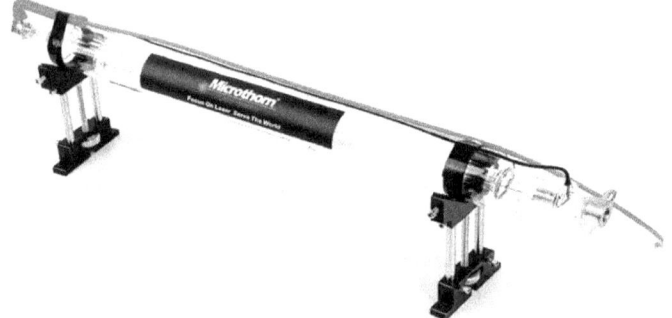

Compare this to the glass water cooled 60 Watt tube at a cost of £400 which is replaced completely after about 1500 hours of use and you can see which is more cost effective for the normal user of these machines. My 40 watt tube in one machine has 2500 hours of use and is still working at 90% capacity but that is probably just down to good maintenance and care.

The basic water cooled CO2 glass laser tube can be fitted to a machine by a reasonably skilled person as it is only brackets to hold it in place and two simple joints sealed with a silicone compound. The sealant is a special silicone compound used to reduce the chance of a high voltage breakdown in the machine.

THE LASER CUTTER HANDBOOK

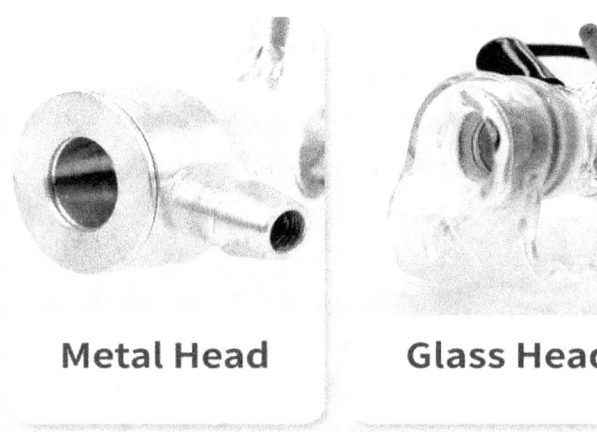

Metal Head   Glass Head

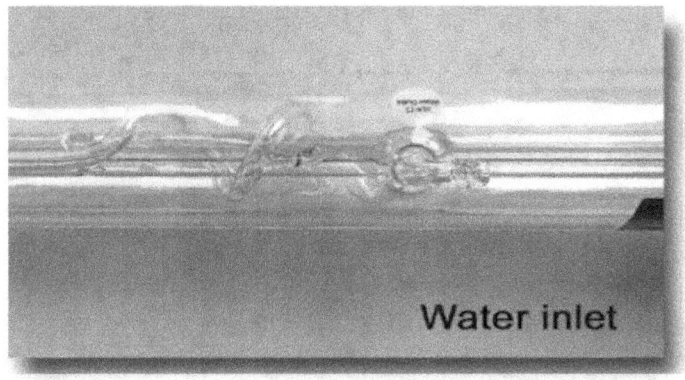

Water inlet

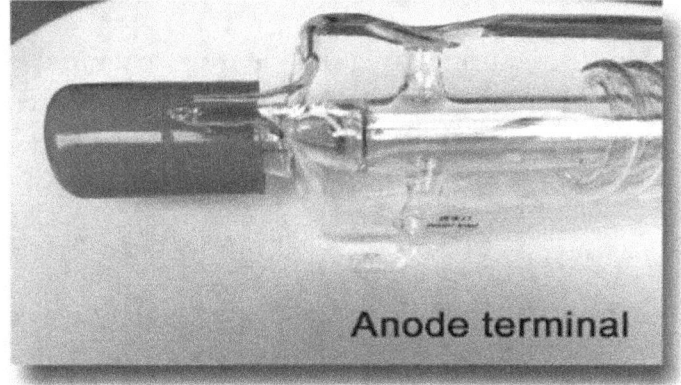

Anode terminal

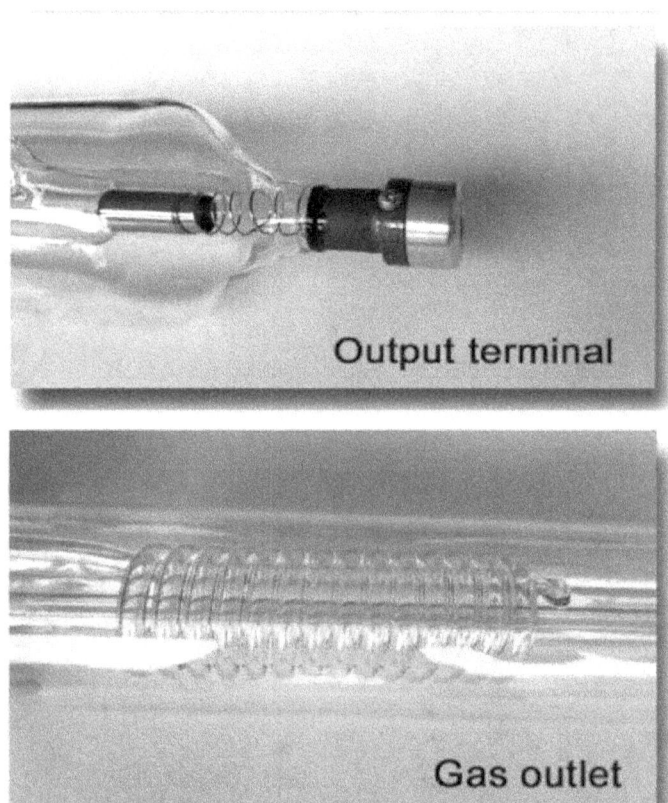

Within the cutting area inside the machine is where the cutting head is mounted onto two mechanical arms or rods; which move with the assistance of electrical motors and chains and belts along the X and Y axis. This is called the gantry and allows for precision movements of the cutting head within a square or rectangular area.

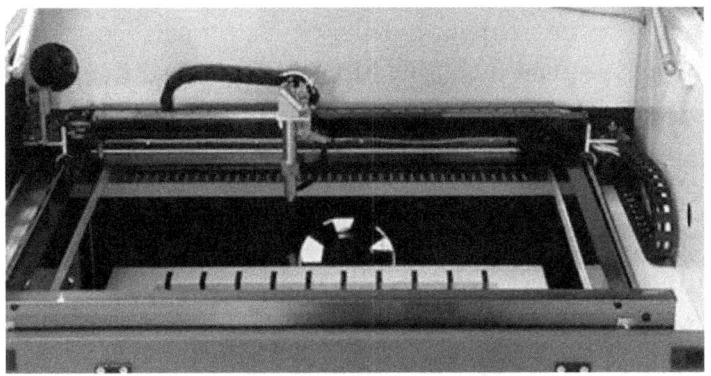

Most of these machines house all the working parts within a metal box with a Perspex viewing panel inserted into the lid.

The main types of lasers used for these machines are :

CO2 lasers

The laser is generated from electrically stimulated gas mixtures (mostly carbon dioxide) and are the most common type of laser because they are lower power; low cost; efficient and can cut and engrave a wide variety of materials.

Wood, paper; leather, acrylic, glass and some plastics.

Neodymium Lasers

Having a much smaller wavelength than Co2 lasers makes for a higher intensity beam and can therefore cut through thicker materials. Quicker to need replaced due to high wear and tear on the machinery.

Can cut metals, plastics and some ceramics.

Fiber Lasers

Similar to neodymium lasers in wavelength and intensity but because of the way they are built they require less maintenance.

Mostly utilized for laser marking processes on metals and plastics.

The software used to control the operation of the machine controls the power; speed; frequency and the resolution to obtain the desired output.

POWER……How strongly the laser fires

SPEED…….. How fast the cutting head moves along the gantry.

FREQUENCY……How fast the laser pulses when the machine is cutting. A higher frequency will make a cleaner cut.

RESOLUTION ….determines the quality of the raster image. Higher resolution creates a darker image on the material.

THE LASER CUTTER HANDBOOK

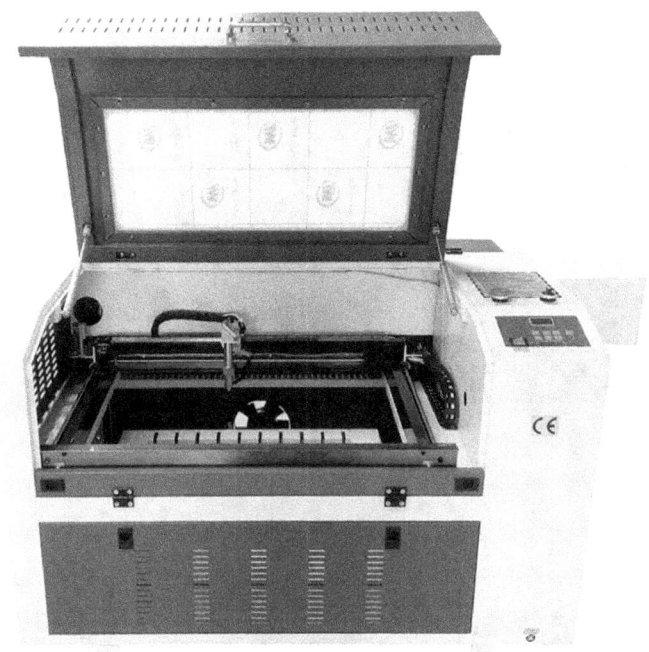

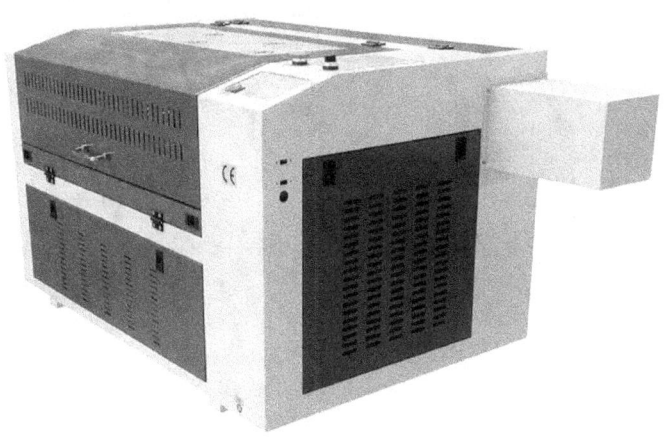

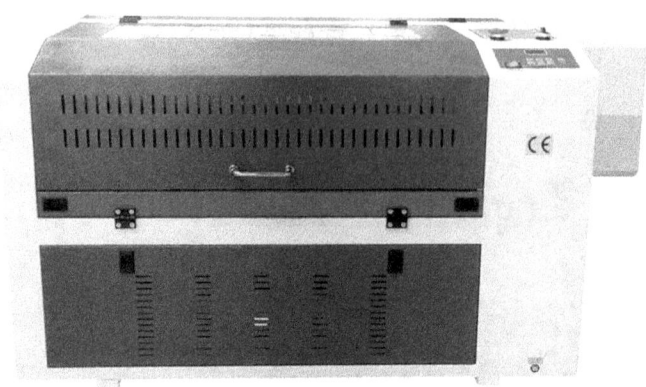

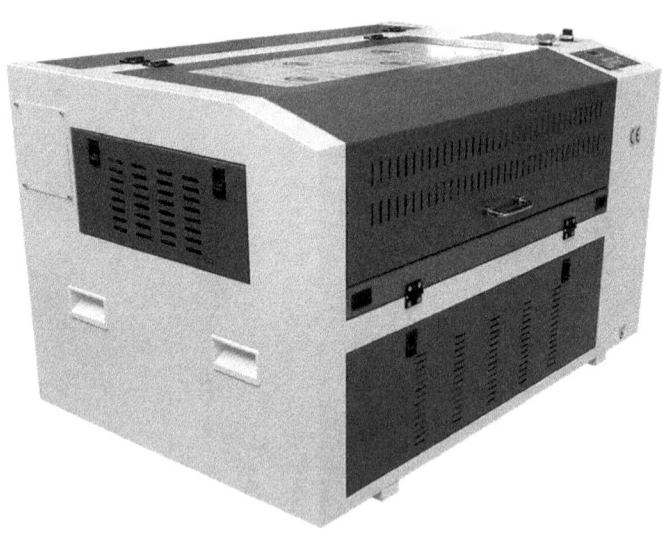

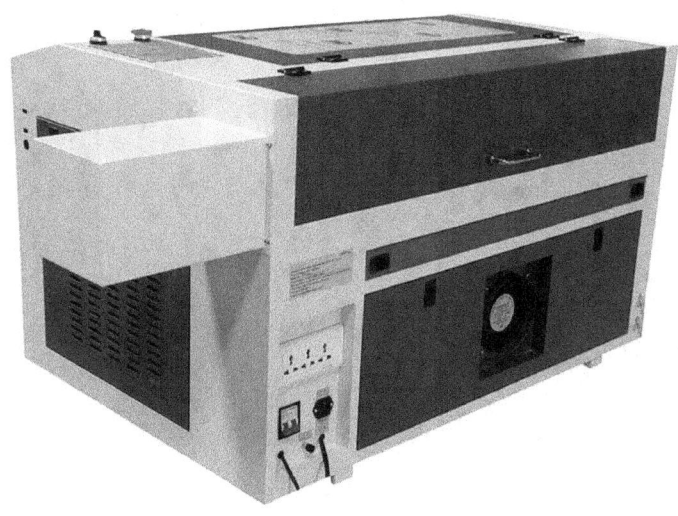

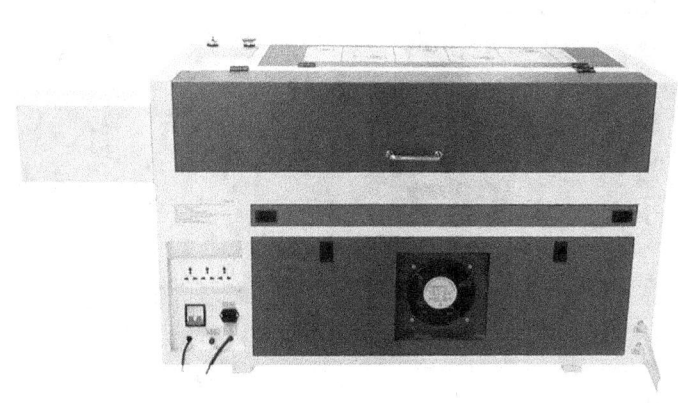

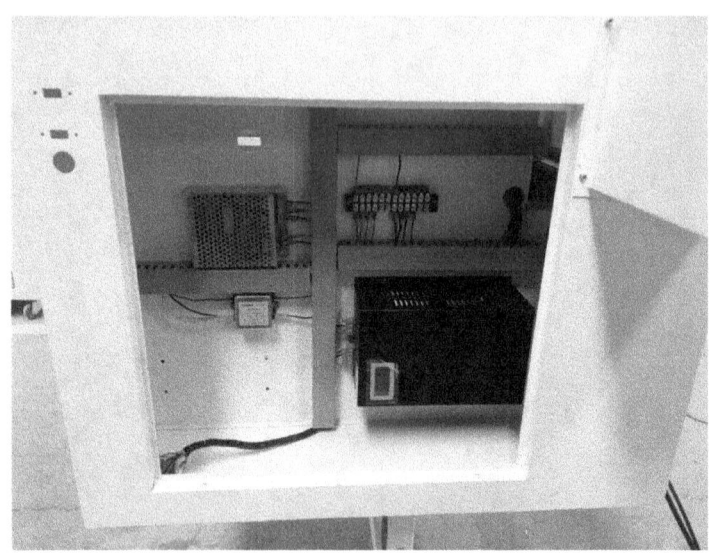

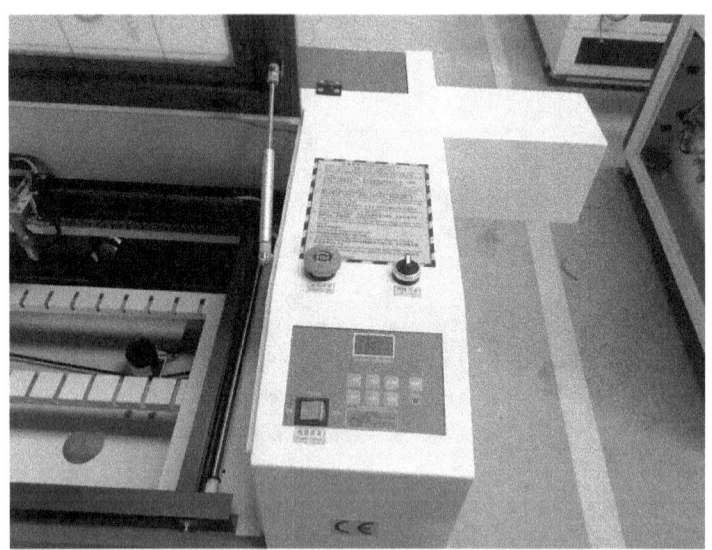

THE LASER CUTTER HANDBOOK

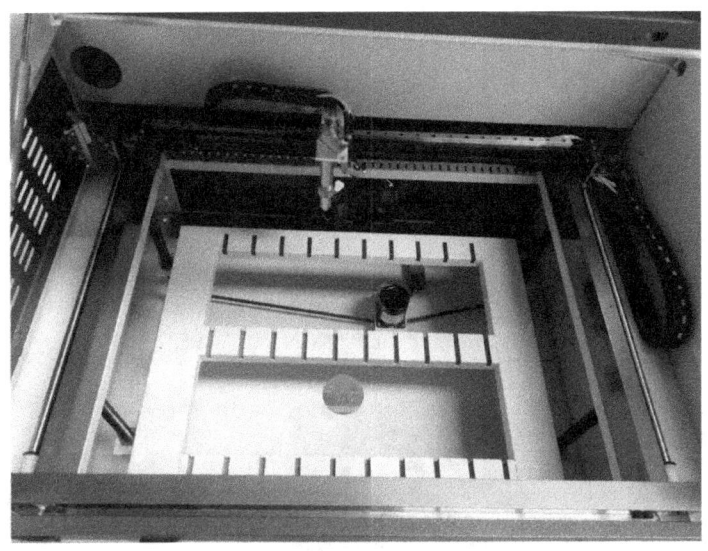

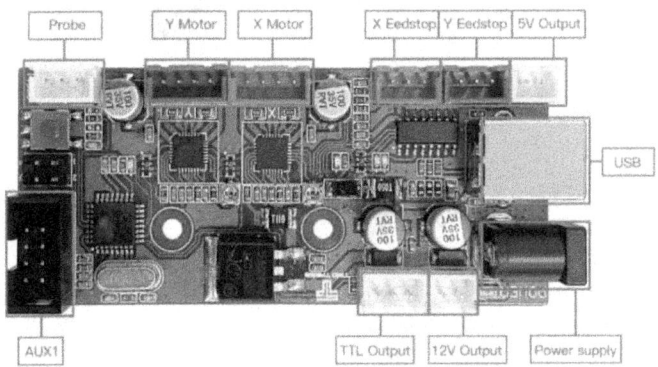

ERIC GOODWIN

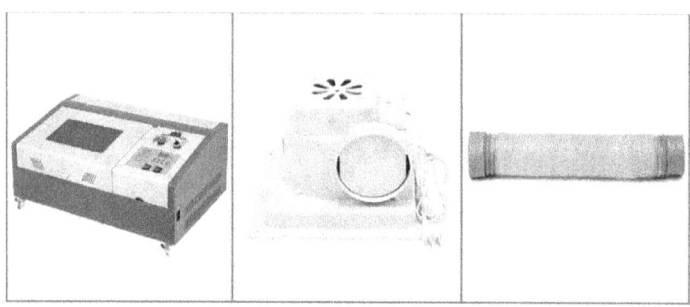

40W LASER ENGRAVER　　EXHAUST FAN　　SMOKE PIPE

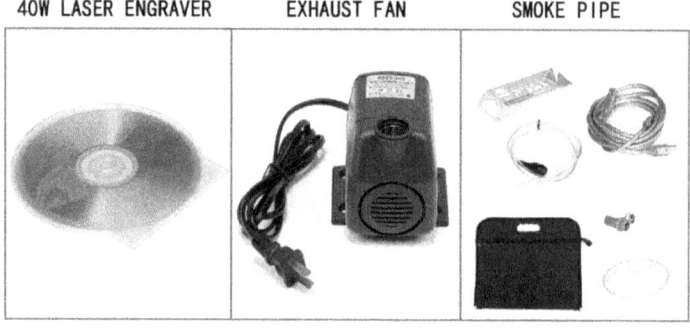

SOFTWARE　　WATER PUMP　　ACCESSORIES

3 – BUYING YOUR FIRST MACHINE

(The Research I did)

Entry level machines cost from GBP£400 and then head north of GBP£25000. My advice on this topic is to buy the machine at the top of your budget if you are intending to use it on a daily basis for several hours, and a lower priced machine if it is for light occasional use.

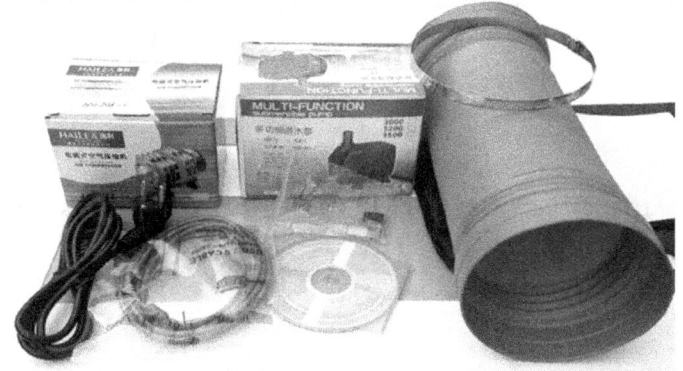

Just bear in mind when you are buying the machine that you will also have to factor in the cost of a cooling system and also an air extraction system and ducting. Not including an air compressor and ancillary tools and equipment.
You definitely need to invest in good quality

machinery if you want to operate hassle free for any length of time. For example the lower cost machines have a cooling system that consists of pump which is immersed into a water container to maintain the laser tube at a safe operating temperature.

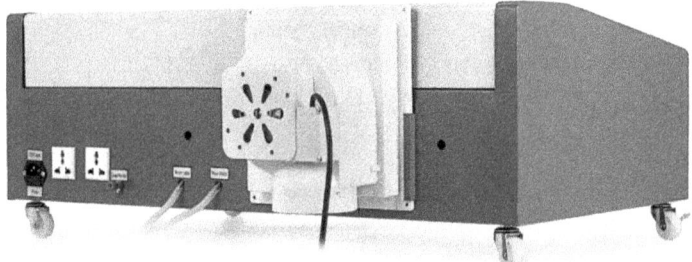

With this system there is very little in the way of environmental control for the temperature, where the more advanced cooling systems will maintain the water temperature within a set range. If for some reason the water rises above the set parameters the machine will automatically shut down until you rectify the problem, thus avoiding any damage to the system.

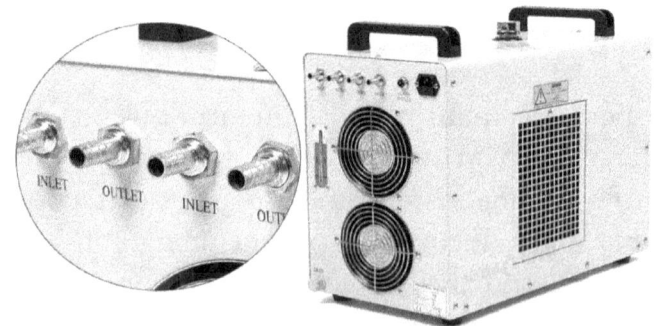

The main question to ask yourself is what will you be using the machinery and equipment for?

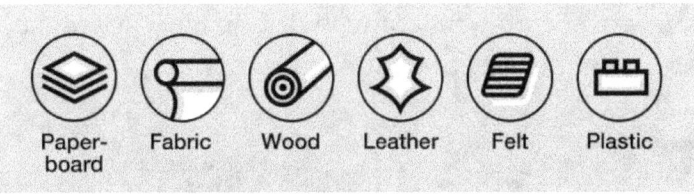

CO2 lasers can be used to cut a wide range of materials at various thicknesses. If you are only cutting paper and card then a small lower powered machine will be sufficient to work at an acceptable level. As an example my 40 watt machine will cleanly cut 3mm acrylic on a single pass. However if you program the machine to make two passes then it will cut 6mm acrylic, with this technique it is possible to cut up to 25mm but the cutting head height will have to be lowered after two passes. So there are ways to create the desired depth of cut without buying the biggest and most powerful machine out there! The wattage for most machines will be in the range of 40 to 60 watts and for most purposes that will be sufficient. It is really down to the quality of the optical lenses that gives the best performance of output.

It is always a good idea to check out customer feedback of previous purchasers of the machine you are considering buying and confirm that it is the same model they are talking about and not some lower cost copy. Ultimately you would want to see the machine working and to make certain that it meets your requirements.

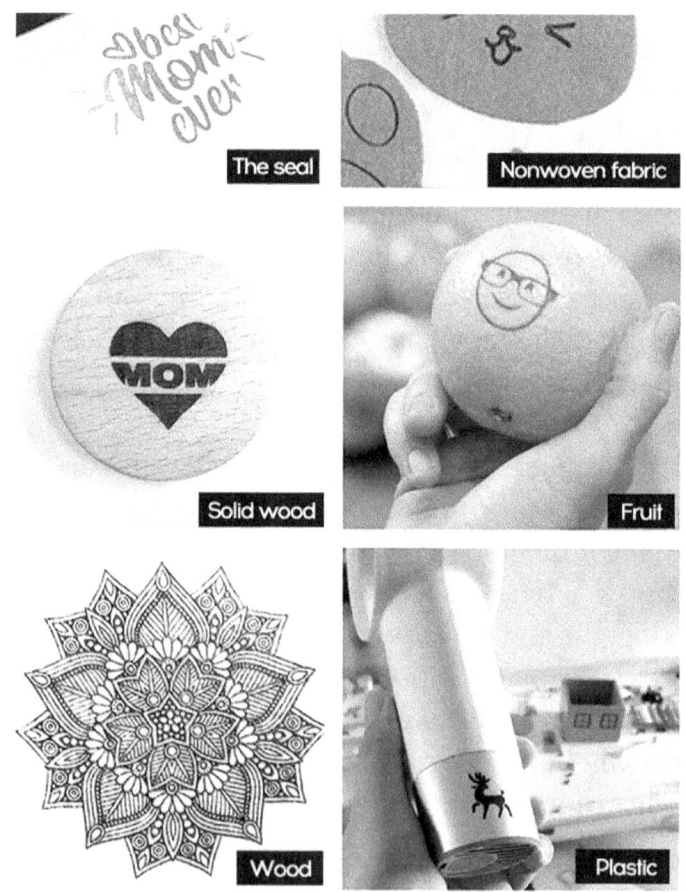

4 – INSTALLING THE MACHINE

Most of the following info is just common sense. Laser Cutters and Engravers emit fumes and heat. These are the main issues that you need to keep in mind when choosing where to place your machine, the cooling system and the Ventilation pipe in your workshop.

Transporting & Unpacking The Machine:
There are components inside your laser cutter that are both delicate & breakable. It only makes sense to be as careful as possible when moving or unpacking the machine.

Choosing The Right Spot:
You'll need plenty of workspace with fairly close access to an outside wall. There is no right or wrong place, just find a good spot that suits you.

Vent Installation:
There really is only two options to vent the fumes from the machine to a safe place.

1) Create a hole in the wall and run the vent pipe through to the outside.

2) Temporarily run the vent pipe outside through an open door or window whenever the machine is in use.

It matters not whichever option you choose, just as long as those nasty fumes are safely extracted and vented outside.

Cooling System Installation:
Your cooling solution does not necessarily need to be right next to your machine, it will be more efficient if it is placed in a cold drafty spot, then it will have less work to do. Depending on the machine in question, some systems are quieter than others. So try to pick a spot that will help to mute a noisy cooler.

Health & Safety:
A birds nest of pipes and cables can be hazardous and will eventually cause problems, so try to keep your install neat & tidy.

5 – THE DESIGN SOFTWARE

To control the output of the machine we have to use software which will manipulate vector graphics. The CO2 laser will use a combination of vector or raster modes and adjustments to power and speed to create the desired designs. Frequency determines how fast the laser pulses during operation and is used only in cutting, and resolution determines the quality of the raster function and only used when rastering.

The rastering process burns off the top layer of the material instead of cutting all the way through as it would in vector mode. Instead of a high powered pulsing beam the machine itself will have a preset lower powered setting which allows the laser machine to spread detailed dots over the face of the material on the cutting bed. By managing the DPI (dots per inch) the raster effect can be controlled to produce different effects on the surface of a material. This technique works well on wood or leather but may not give the desired effect on other materials, that's why it is always useful to use a test piece first before destroying valuable materials.

Vector mode is used mainly for cutting materials such as Acrylic and MDF, but can be used to engrave lines by adjusting the power down to a lower setting. If you create your design in the software I recommend, then you can set the line output to hairline which the machine treats as a vector line and will therefore work in cut mode. (0.005 inch) or (0.127mm). Anything above this size will be treated as raster mode which will allow for different dpi settings in the same way as a normal inkjet printer would work.

Vector engraving is also known as "kiss cuts". It provides a method to follow vector lines but only cuts into the surface of the material on the cutting bed. You cannot vary the thickness of the laser beam without changing out the focusing lens, as the beam is a fixed width. However, you can achieve different results by varying the height of the cutting head distance from the material which in turn alters the resulting track width on the surface of the material. Remember that to fill an area in on your work piece you use the engraving settings to make the laser beam go back and forth over an area moving down by the width of the laser beam until the area is covered. This makes some projects not only time consuming but also costly to produce.

To work with any level of efficiency you must have a basic understanding of vector graphics ; vector shapes and vector objects. These are made up of lines and curves defined by mathematical objects called vectors, which describe a given image according to its geometrical characteristics. It is easy to modify vector graphics without losing detail and that is why they are used for manipulating designs for the laser cutting process.

As you draw a line using drawing software you are creating a path. The path consisting of one or more straight or curved segments. The start and finish of each segment are marked by anchor points or nodes which work like pins holding a wire in position, so allowing the user to left mouse click onto a node and drag it to a new position thus changing its shape or you can also delete it.

The node will usually change colour when

selected, you can also select multiple nodes at the same time for manipulation.

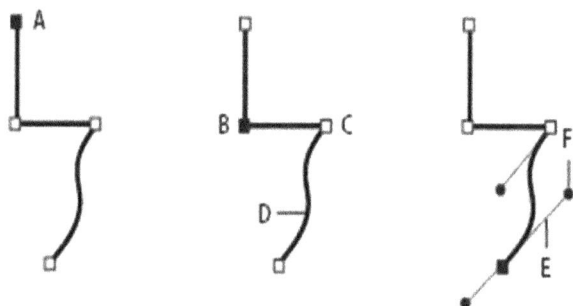

Components of a path.
   A. Selected endpoint.
   B. Selected anchor or node point.
   C. Unselected node.
   D. Curved path segment.
   E. Direction line for adjustment.
   F. Direction point paths consist of corner points and smooth points. At a corner point a path abruptly changes direction.

At a smooth points the path segments are connected as a continuous curve. A combination of these can be used to create a path and can also be changed to the required point.

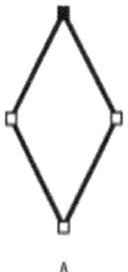 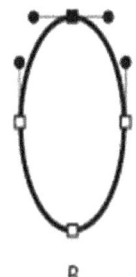 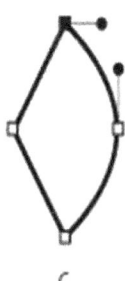

A   B   C

Points of a path

- A. 4 corner points.
- B. 4 smooth points.
- C. Combination of smooth and corner points.
- D. A corner point can connect any two straight or curved segments, but a smooth point always connects two curved segments.

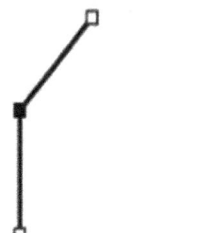 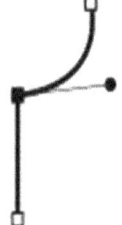 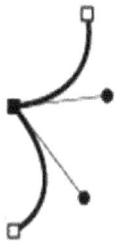

A corner point can connect straight and curved segments.

There are many software packages out there to use for creating the designs for your laser cutting projects but the ones listed below are the main ones I would use on a regular basis.

For 2D design use CorelDraw which is a graphic design software with an extensive number of tools and applications and more importantly it is easy to use.

Adobe Illustrator and Photoshop are both powerful software packages which can be used to create high quality designs. They are also useful for converting images into different formats.

AutoCAD is free for students and used a lot by engineers and architects to create detailed drawings and product representations.

Inkscape is a free open source graphic design software which I find most useful and would encourage you to donate something if you are going to use it to allow them to keep up their good work.

For 3D design the main contenders are both from Solidworks, who produce Engineering software. They are 'Solidworks Autodesk Inventor' and 'Solidworks Autodesk fusion'.

Autodesk Inventor is free for students and is a professional mechanical design software.

Autodesk Fusion is also free to students but is a cloud based platform to help designers through the whole design process. Apart from all the various software packages the laser cutter machine will also have its own software that basically acts in the same way as a printer driver does except that it will also have basic design capabilities. It is the interface between user and machine that will allow you to create simple designs and implement directly to the machine. My recommendation is to carry out all your design work out within Photoshop; CorelDraw and Inkscape then save the file as a DXF format and import it using the machines software for implementation.

How to use these software programs.

Method A

Create your design in CorelDraw and save as a DXF file to the desktop then go to your laser cutter software and import the file to use.

Resize your design to the required specifications and run the print cut option. Remember when creating your design in CorelDraw to use the hairline option to create lines for cutting anything other than this will tell the machine to engrave or raster.

Method B

Use this method if you want to create a design file from an image. (.png or .jpeg)

Try to select a good quality black and white image with clear lines as this will convert easily to DXF.

To convert more complex images you would have to first open it in CorelDraw or Photoshop and remove all the parts of the image not required then save it as a black and white BITMAP. Next open the file in

Inkscape and be sure to select the image. At the top of the page use the trace bitmap feature to create an SVG (scalable vector graphic). A more in depth tutorial can be found on YOUTUBE but the basics are:

PATH
TRACE BITMAP

Select either (edge detection) or brightness cutoff and then play around with the threshold settings until you get a good result in the preview panel in inkscape. Once you are happy with the result click OK.

Inkscape will create a vector graphic which can take up to a minute or so depending on the file size but once it has finished you are left with an SVG. If it was a complicated image then you will probably get more lines and curves than you wanted but it is just a matter of selecting what is not required and deleting them before saving to the desktop as a DXF file.

Once the file is in DXF format it can be imported into your laser cutter software for use.

6 – RUNNING A TEST PROJECT

Once all your equipment is connected together the main concern is that the cooling system has the correct level of water with the additive in it. Follow the fitting instructions for your particular machine and then visually check the glass tube does not have any air bubbles in the water as this will cause overheating in the tube. If you find there are bubbles then pinch one of the feed tubes repeatedly in a pumping motion until you dislodge the bubble. The cooling system will have to be running to completer this task.

Once this has all been corrected the next thing to do is align all the mirror lenses in the flying optics system.

Diagram 1.

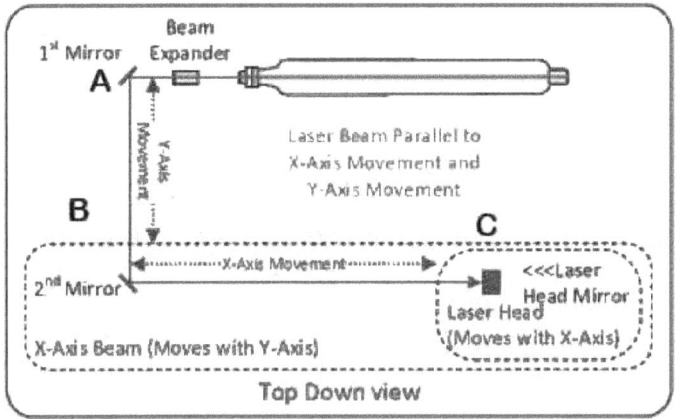

Diagram 2

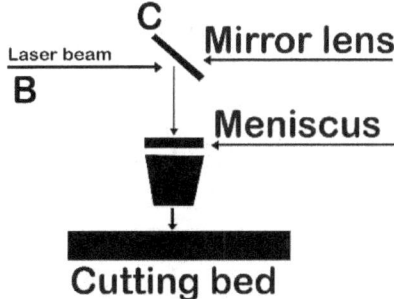

Always start the alignment process with the mirror closest to the firing end of the glass laser tube. There will be adjustment screws at the side or rear of the mirror lens which will move the lens from side to side or up and down. Turn the screws in increments of 1mm as these small movements will allow you to align the beam correctly. Aim to have the beam hit the exact centre of the mirror. If your alignment is out and the laser beam hits the side of the lens then it will cause beam scatter. You can confirm that beam scatter is occurring as the laser will cut two lines in your material instead of just a single line.

As the beam is not visible to the human eye you will need to tape a piece of white card over each mirror so that when you fire the laser it will mark a single small circle on the card to show where it is hitting. I usually mark the centre of the mirror on the card with a pencil to show if I am on target.

In the above diagram it shows a typical layout of the flying optics, so in this example you would start at point A then once that mirror lens if correctly adjusted you would move to point B and repeat the card alignment process until you progress to the cutting head.

At the cutting head there is a hole or aperture where the beam enters the cutting head housing C in diagram 2. To hit the final mirror at this point you just tape card over the hole to find the centre of that mirror.

If you need to you can move the cutting head closer to the previous mirror to make alignment easier. Just reduce the power to 70% and position the cutting head housing approximately 150mm away from the lens B diagram 1.

Make the adjustments using the screws and remember to remove the card each time. Sometime you have to clean the lens as the card can produce smoke which will cover the lens and reduce performance.

NB. A rule of thumb is if the spot on the card needs to move up then tilt the mirror up using the adjustment screws and the same process for moving the burn spot on the card down.
All laser cutting systems will have a focusing procedure to ensure that the laser beam cuts to its full potential. Even a 1mm misalignment can make a difference to performance bearing in mind that they usually operate to a tolerance of 0.01mm.

7 – TOOLS & EQUIPMENT

Your Computer:
The software programs you will need can be quite resource hungry when working on complicated tasks. There may be times when you will be flicking back and forth between several quite powerful software programs. For this reason I recommend that you use a fairly powerful computer if possible. Otherwise you will experience unwanted lag and screen freezes that will stifle your productivity.

The easiest way to avoid those issues is to use a computer that is up to the task. Older generation PC's and low powered laptops may not be powerful enough for the job at hand, so here's a few recommendations to solve these issues.

Buy a new PC. I say this with trepidation, as there are some real bad ones out there that even from new; that will not be good enough for the purpose. If you choose this route I recommend the following minimum specification.

AMD or Intel?
The latest generation of AMD Ryzen CPU's & APU's are light years ahead of Intel and will be upgradable in the future. The latest 10 & 11th Generation of Intel CPU's are good, but are less power efficient than the equivalent AMD CPU, and the Intel chips are more expensive.

AMD CPU:
Minimum Ryzen 5 or 7. My own recommendation is AMD Ryzen 5 3600X or 5600x if you can stretch to the latest release.

INTEL CPU:
Minimum Intel I5 or I7 (8th Gen).

RAM: A minimum of 8GB of DDR4 ram is needed for Windows 10 to run at a reasonable pace. I'd recommend 16GB of DDR4 3200 in dual channel mode (2x8GB) for running multiple power hungry applications.

HDD:

There are still new PC's being sold with old style spinning hard drives in speeds of 5400rpm or 7200 rpm, but they are all too slow for your purposes, so be sure that your new PC comes with either a newer SSD (Solid State Disk) which are 3x faster, or an NVME SSD, which can be from 10x to 40x faster than a spinning hard drive.

If you want a responsive computer, then NVME is the way to go. Your computer will boot up in seconds and programs will open instantly. Don't be palmed off with older technology that's not fit for purpose.

GRAPHICS:
Onboard graphics will not really be powerful enough for running graphics intensive software programs. The solution is a mid-range graphics card. Modern graphics cards can get pretty expensive, but unless you're playing games on your tea-break, you won't need to spend too much money on one. Any modern 4GB graphics card will be good enough for most scenarios. I use a Radeon RX560X that cost a mere £150.

Upgrade Your Old PC: The computer you already have might well be fine for our purposes, or it may just need a boost to give it some extra poke. If your PC is not that old, just adding some

RAM and an SSD can produce the boost you need. If you're currently using onboard graphics, just adding a graphics card along with an SSD can make a world of difference.

Laptops:
It might come as a surprise to learn that most laptops may not be powerful enough to run those software programs without severe lag. If you really must have a laptop, then opt for something with an Intel i5 or i7 CPU (10th or 11th generation), or an AMD Ryzen 5 or 7 CPU. Modern AMD laptops tend to have more power coupled with stronger onboard graphics. My own recommendation would be anything with an AMD 3500U or higher CPU.

Apple Mac:
Modern Macbooks, IMAC's & Mac Pro's tend to be quite powerful machines, so if that's what you have, it will probably be fine, provided it is running an SSD and not an old style spinning hard drive. There is usually a Mac compatible version available for all of the previously mentioned software programs.

CO2 Laser Cutting Machine:
Position the machine so that it is easily accessible with at least 300mm clearance around the outside

of the machine.

The Extractor:
You'll need an extraction unit or fume filter unit to safely ventilate the fumes via ducting pipes to the outside. The fume filter extracts fumes to help reduce the amount of hazardous contaminates introduced into the air and this then helps protect the machine user from health issues. The fumes can blur the laser beam and effect cutting efficiency.

LEV = Local Exhaust Ventilation
LGAC = Laser Generated Air Contaminates

One water chiller unit which will pump water around the outside of the glass tube to keep it from overheating.

Remember to add the antifreeze additive
(LS Coolflow additive) which will prevent the water from freezing and also the build up of algae.

Small air compressor as an air assist which directs a stream of air over the work surface at the cutting head to control heat.

Software packages. Either Photoshop or Corel

draw and Inkscape plus the software that controls the laser machine. (See chapter 6 for further details).

Tool Kit
Small electrical screwdriver.
Adjustable spanner.
Allen keys.
Optical cleaning paper.
Cotton buds.
Isopropyl alcohol.
Silicone spray.
White card 200gsm.
Non-perfumed baby wipes.
Small plastic scraper.
Safety glasses.
Acrylic measuring gauge, for measuring the distance between head and work-piece. Spares can be easily made with laser cutter.

Roller attachment for cutting cylindrical items. (optional).
Hot Wire bending machine (optional). Although not a requirement to operate the machine I have found that it is an essential piece of equipment for bending acrylic when forming angles in the acrylic.

Materials – Cast Acrylic; mdf; laser-ply; card and

paper.

CO 2 lasers cut all the above but remember they are all flammable and can go on fire in seconds.

NEVER LEAVE THE MACHINE UNATTENDED!

I have listed suppliers of the products I use at the back of this book.

If you intend to cut or engrave plastics then you need to be certain that they do not contain PVC . Chlorine gas is produced which is highly toxic and corrosive to both human and machine. If in doubt find the MSDS (material safety data sheet) for your material and be 100% sure you know what it is made from. Chlorinated plastics burn with a hint of green to the flame.

If you want to cut mirrored cast acrylic then always cut from the back of the material and also cover with lining paper that has been slightly dampened with water. This prevents the back becoming destroyed with smoke from the cutting process.

8 – ESSENTIAL MAINTENANCE

If the machine you are using is working to an acceptable standard, then leave well alone until you start noticing a reduction in cutting power!

Many problems that arise in a computer system are caused by the accumulation of dirt and dust. Those problems will get worse over time due to the lack of every day cleaning and maintenance. Your laser cutter will suffer the same fate if you don't keep it clean.

Cleaning Schedule:
Ensure that you create a maintenance schedule for daily; weekly and monthly checks.

Work Area:

You must keep a clean work area within and around the machine. My experience has been that the machine will do its best to set something on fire, given the opportunity.

Isolate The Mains:

When working on maintaining the machine try to get into the habit of completely disconnecting it from the power source before starting any work.

Lubrication:

Lubricate the gantry runners and bearings with silicone spray at regular intervals to stop damage caused by friction. The use of mineral oils will degrade nylon bearings!

Cleaning:

Cleaning your machine is an essential task that will make a huge difference to the performance of your machine. These cleaning duties comprise of the following tasks.

Cleaning The Casing:

Wipe down the inside and outside of the machine with a lint free cloth.

Cleaning the Cutting Bed:

Vacuum out any loose material from within the

cutting bed area. The cutting bed can be cleaned with a plastic scraper and unscented baby wipes. Using baby wipes will prevent the promotion of rust.

Cleaning The Lens Mirrors:
Cleaning of the lens mirrors within the flying optics system must be carried out very carefully, as a movement of 1mm will have a negative effect on the cutting ability of the laser cutter.

Use virgin cotton buds dipped in isopropyl alcohol. Start with gentle circular motions from the center of the lens working outwards. Make sure to change the cotton buds often so that you do not cause any scratches on the lens as this will cause the laser beam to scatter. Once the lens is clean and dry use optical paper with circular motions go give the mirror lens a final polish.

The last lens to be cleaned is located in the cutting head housing and is nearest the cutting bed. It is a coloured lens called a meniscus and this it what will focus the beam. It has a convex face which must face in the correct direction for it to function correctly. It is cleaned in the same manner as all the other lenses but you just have to take note of how it is placed within the housing.

If you're cutting a lot of MDF then the lens will gather smut or smoke residue, this is best cleaned off first with a cotton bud and de-ionized water before carrying out the cleaning procedure.

Cleaning The Extraction Filters:
Any filters and ducting for the air extraction unit will need cleaned out with a vacuum on a weekly basis, be sure to wear a face mask to prevent inhalation of dust.

Overview:
High speed engraving for long periods of time will create wear and tear on the machine and also a lot of contaminated particles. You will need to increase the intervals for your maintenance schedule if this is the case.

9 – TROUBLESHOOTING

The speed and power settings are dictated by the type of material you are cutting. It is good practice to make a list of what speed and power setting get the best results for a particular material as this will save time for future work being carried out. Harder thicker materials require higher power and a slower speed to complete a successful cut while a thinner material can be cut using lower power and a higher speed so to ensure that you don't get burn damage on the material.

Small features or details in a project in a concentrated area can cause localized heat build up which might cause the material to melt or catch fire. If you have to cut parallel lines then try to leave at least a 2mm between each line as this should help prevent damage.

1. Load file into laser cutting software and prepare to run the selected program.

2. Switch on laser cutter and all other attached equipment. Ensure that is connected correctly and full functional.

3. Load material onto the cutting bed of the machine.

4. Use your measuring template to confirm the cutting head position is at the correct distance away from the material as specified in your manual for your specific machine.

5. Run program and monitor laser while in operation.

6. On completion of cutting program remove the material from the cutting bed and clean out any offcuts left behind.

7. Turn off machine completely if not in use.

Breakages:

Most parts produced with a laser cutter using Wood or Acrylic will tend to break easily. It is standard practice to create various joints so as to strengthen your product for use.

Finger Joints: These come in all shapes and sizes and are useful for joining two flat pieces of material together at a perpendicular angle to make a corner. It basically consists of tabs on each side of the material that interlock and are usually as long as it is thick to make a clean seam.

Mortice and Tenon Joints: These are similar to finger joints except the fingers of one piece protrude through holes in the other piece to be joined together. Useful for creating T like structures and also for mounting internal supports.

Slotted Joints: These are two connecting pieces which each have slots cut halfway through them which then slide into each other to form an X shape.

Dovetail and Jigsaw Joints: These are usually used to mount two materials flush to one another.

10 – GET CREATIVE

I mainly produce my own products from MDF; laser-ply or cast acrylic. These cut easily and are cheap to buy in quantity. I then either sell them wholesale to retailers, or retail them myself online in the more popular selling websites.

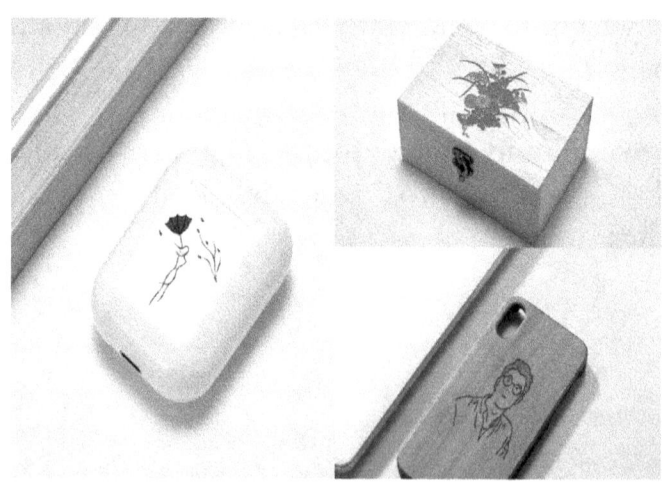

THE LASER CUTTER HANDBOOK

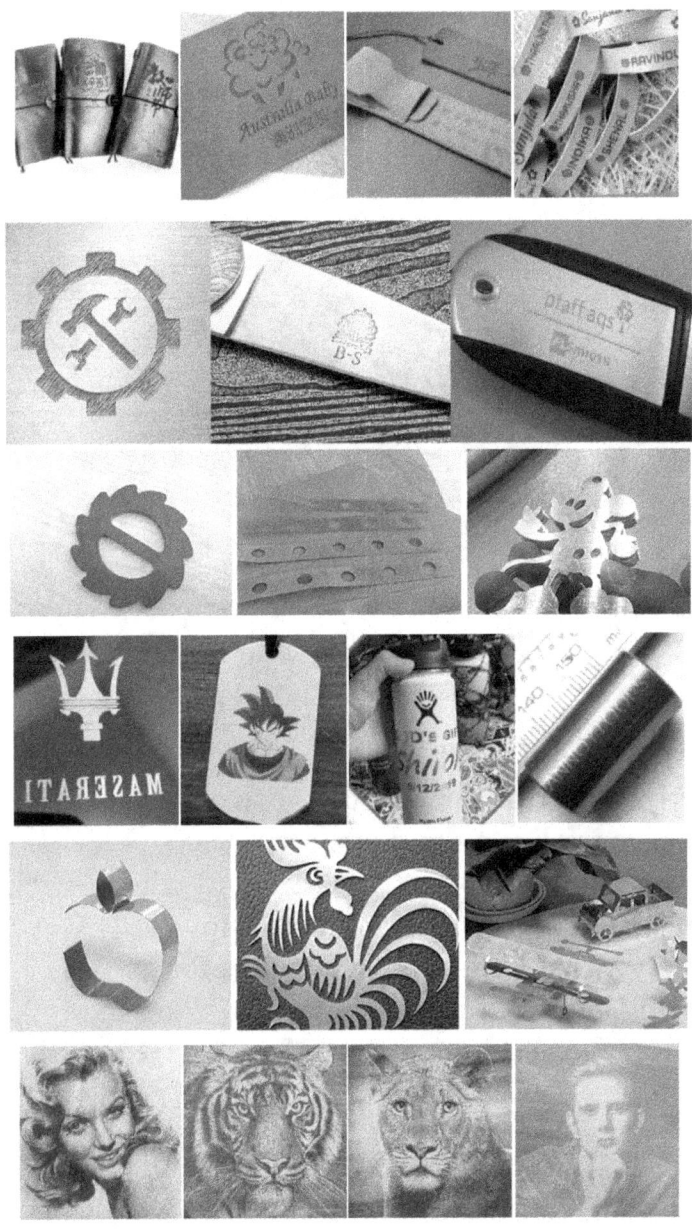

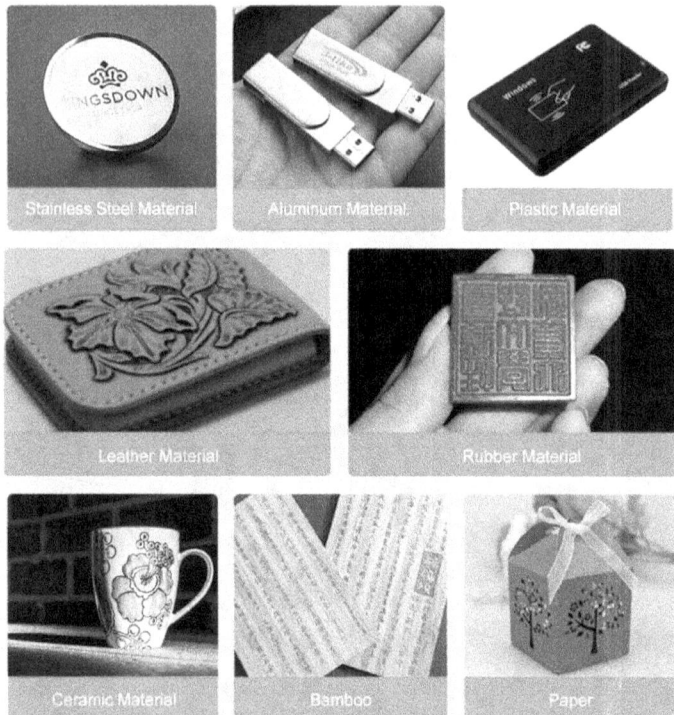

If you can create unique and original products then you will soon find that it is fairly straightforward to find customers. My first original product that I produced with a laser cutter was a simple acrylic template for the baking industry I then marketed it online and within six weeks I was selling 800 units a month.

The income from that single product was in the region of GBP£4000 a month and it was still selling 200 units a month five years later.

I currently have 52 different products online selling in similar numbers. Now you can see how a simple idea for a product can turn a laser cutter into a money making machine.

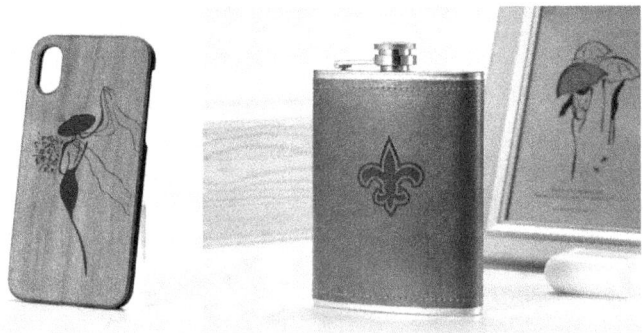

There are many different materials and manufacturing methods available for producing your ideas. You only need to be willing to take the initiative and use your creative ability to produce sellable products. I've spent the last ten years proving it works. Just create your own range of products, then find some hungry buyers on Amazon, eBay or Etsy, then you too can build a very lucrative business.

11 USEFUL LINKS

www.Hindleys.com
www.kitronic.co.uk
www.hpclaser.co.uk

ABOUT THE AUTHOR

Eric Goodwin currently lives in the United Kingdom, where he runs several businesses in the craft industry. He is happily married to Barbara and is the proud father of three children.

www.ingramcontent.com/pod-product-compliance
Lightning Source LLC
Chambersburg PA
CBHW070459220526
45466CB00004B/1886